J. Rooker, manatee

told by:
Jan Haley

painted by:
Paul Brent

FOCUS
PUBLISHING, INC.

Focus Publishing, Inc.
502 Third Street NW
Bemidji, MN 56601

J. Rooker, Manatee

Printed in Korea

Publisher's Cataloging in Publication

Haley, Jan
    J. Rooker, manatee/told by Jan Haley; painted by Paul Brent.

    p. cm.
    ISBN: 1-885904-29-0
    SUMMARY: A manatee of the southwest Florida coast is
injured, then rescued, rehabilitated, and returned to the wild.
Based on a true story.

    1. Manatees - Juvenile literature. I. Title

QL737. S63H35 1996   599.5'5
                             QB195-20641

Lovingly dedicated to
Ferne
for her enduring faith in me.

Jan Haley

I dedicate the illustrations in this book
to my sons,
Jensen and Anders
who are a constant source of inspiration to me.

Paul Brent

Preface

The waters of the Gulf of Mexico stroke the southwestern tip of Florida, warming the many waterways (some natural, some man-made) that etch its shoreline. In these marine habitats, or estuaries, fresh water from rivers, streams, and springs mingles with salt water from the ocean, making their brackish waters inviting sanctuaries for an abundance of ocean life. In fact, these canals and marinas, bays and lagoons are among the most highly productive ecosystems on earth.

One of these sanctuaries is Rookery Bay National Estuarine Research Reserve near Marco Island, Florida. Henderson Creek, Rookery Bay's main freshwater source, extends three miles or more inland from the coast. At one point, it narrows to a quiet, slow, meandering canal. At the end of this canal is a secluded lagoon surrounded by mangrove trees. Springs boil up from the bottom of the lagoon, supplying fresh water and a constant temperature in times of cold weather. The lagoon is a peaceful place; at high tide, the low-hanging limbs of the mangroves slap gently at the water.

To the casual observer, the lagoon appears to be nothing more than a stagnant pond. Those who look closely, however, see much more.

Each year as many as twelve manatees make their way into the lagoon. They munch contentedly in this watery pasture, rest along its bottom, and float along its surface. They swim into inland waterways like this one in search of warmer waters. The manatees are social animals, so perhaps one follows another. One thing is certain. A visit from the manatee is a gift from the sea.

As a Minnesota native, I didn't know what a manatee looked like until I visited Florida and saw one at Disney's Epcot Center. I felt an immediate bond with this charming, vulnerable mammal, and sought to learn more about it.

One of the things I learned is that more manatees die each year than are born. Manatees have no natural predators; their greatest enemy is man. Because manatees move so slowly, they can't always get out of the way when motorboats speed by. The sharp, whirling propellers of a boat can cut them as they swim just below the surface of the water. Infection can set into these deep cuts. Many wounded manatees die.

Later, I met the manatees of Henderson Creek. There I witnessed the rescue of one who had been wounded. He was given the name "J. Rooker" because he was rescued near Rookery Bay. He

was rehabilitated and tattooed with a number "43" so he could be tracked after his release.

As we learn more about manatees, or other endangered animals, I think we find a higher level of concern for their protection. When I came to know J. Rooker, in particular, I knew that I needed to share his story.

Long before he had a name, before he had a number, J. Rooker had a home. Secure in the nearness of his mother, he swam and frolicked with her in the vast warm waters of the sea. He never was one to wander very far from her side.

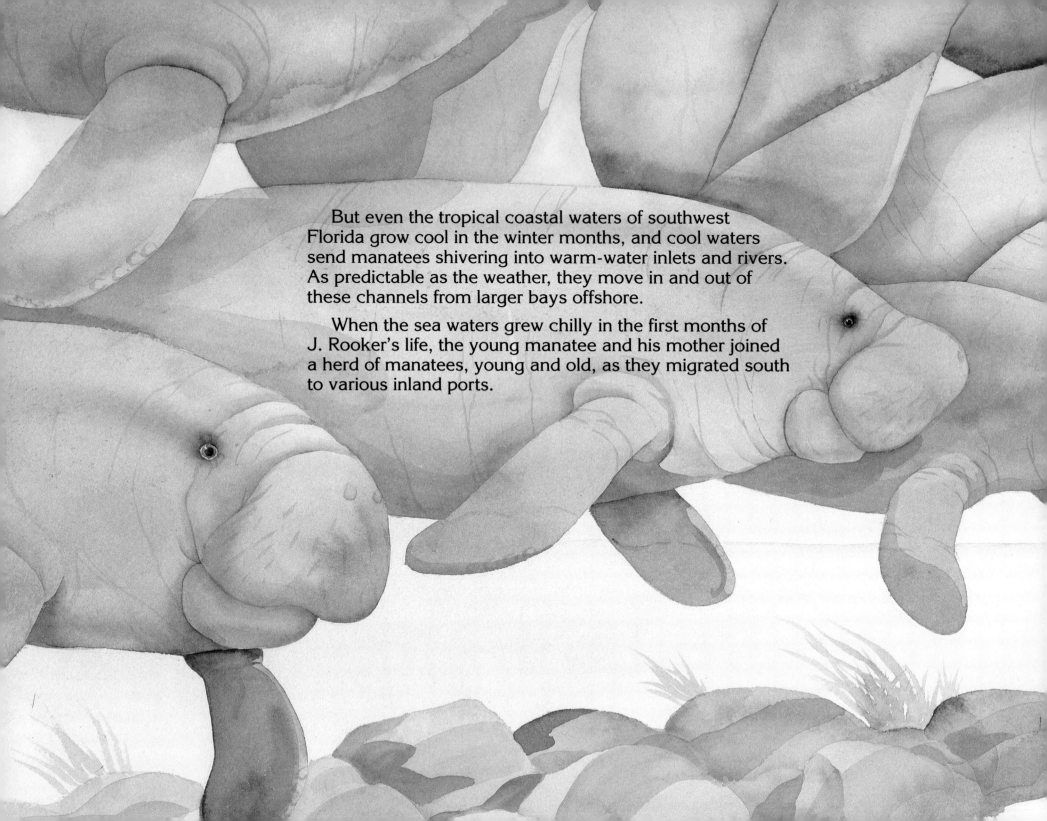

But even the tropical coastal waters of southwest Florida grow cool in the winter months, and cool waters send manatees shivering into warm-water inlets and rivers. As predictable as the weather, they move in and out of these channels from larger bays offshore.

When the sea waters grew chilly in the first months of J. Rooker's life, the young manatee and his mother joined a herd of manatees, young and old, as they migrated south to various inland ports.

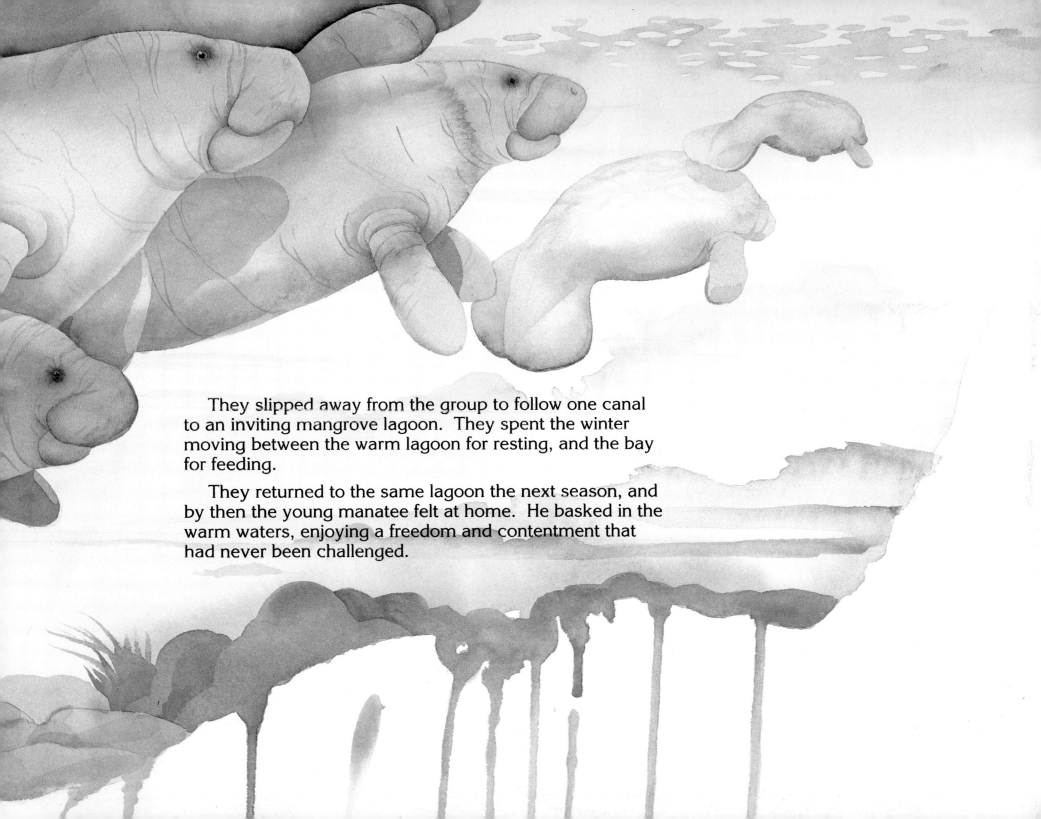

They slipped away from the group to follow one canal to an inviting mangrove lagoon. They spent the winter moving between the warm lagoon for resting, and the bay for feeding.

They returned to the same lagoon the next season, and by then the young manatee felt at home. He basked in the warm waters, enjoying a freedom and contentment that had never been challenged.

In the autumn of his third season, as he returned from the sea with his mother, that tranquility was shattered. About two miles off Rookery Bay, the ocean waters heaved and rolled. Sand, muck, plants, and bits of debris swirled and clouded his vision. Then, as suddenly as it hit, the turmoil ended. His mother was gone. He went on alone, certain to meet her again at the lagoon. She never arrived.

Now, the motherless manatee pushes his whiskered nose out of the water and exhales, making a soft "whoosh" as he dives back down. Though only a few years old, he already has barnacle tattoos, the tiny marks left by crustaceans that attach and grow on a manatee's thick hide in salt water. The barnacles have fallen off because they cannot live in fresh water, but their marks remain.

He has been foraging quietly on the bottom near several other manatees who are resting nearby. Each time he surfaces, the water feels soothingly warm. His back briefly skims the air as he stretches and dives forward and down once again. The bright sunshine makes him squint his small, blubbery eyes. Moving to the bottom once more, he pokes one last bite of water hyacinth into his mouth and settles for a rest.

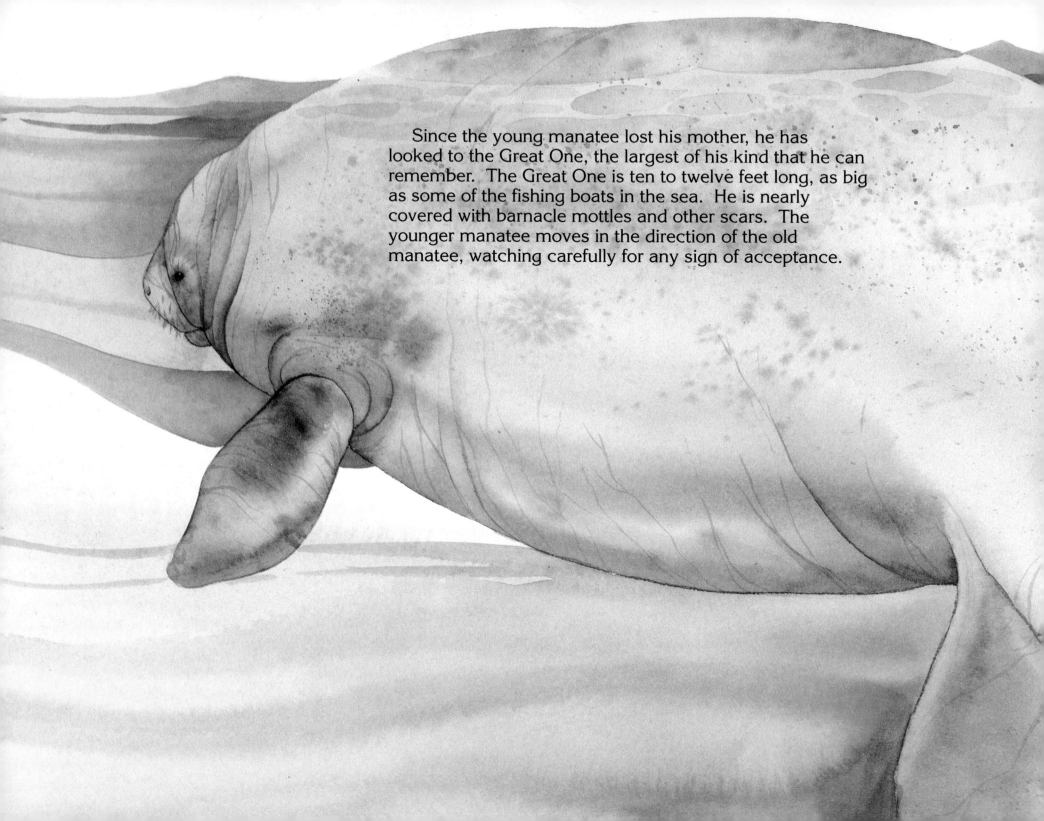

Since the young manatee lost his mother, he has looked to the Great One, the largest of his kind that he can remember. The Great One is ten to twelve feet long, as big as some of the fishing boats in the sea. He is nearly covered with barnacle mottles and other scars. The younger manatee moves in the direction of the old manatee, watching carefully for any sign of acceptance.

Finally, he moves closer, nuzzling the Great One and reaching out with his flippers. The Great One never responds, and he slides slowly away. The Great One is unapproachable to the persistently sociable calf. Each time the young manatee moves close to him, the Great One quietly withdraws.

Swimming alone one day, the young manatee slowly makes his way into the canal leading to the lagoon. The sun is bright, and he swims lazily just beneath the surface. Suddenly, some great thing assaults him with an impact that pushes him downward in a mighty surge of water and foam.

A penetrating pain shoots through him, as if his back has been ripped open, which in fact it has. He is stunned. Somehow he had missed the familiar sound of the power-boat. He hears it now as it roars away.

Feeling himself bob up again in the powerboat's wake, he struggles to find protection on the bottom. The pain is almost unbearable. The thick hide of his back has ripped apart where the propeller of the motorboat has slashed him. He floats on the surface of the murky water and slips into a drowsy, half-conscious state. The pain eases slightly.

Growing weaker, he closes his eyes and struggles toward the lagoon. When he finally finds himself there, he sinks to the bottom. Pain consumes him. He sleeps.

By the time night has fallen, he is unable to return to the bottom for safety. When he tries to submerge, he bounces uncontrollably back to the surface, tail-first. His breathing is ragged and labored.

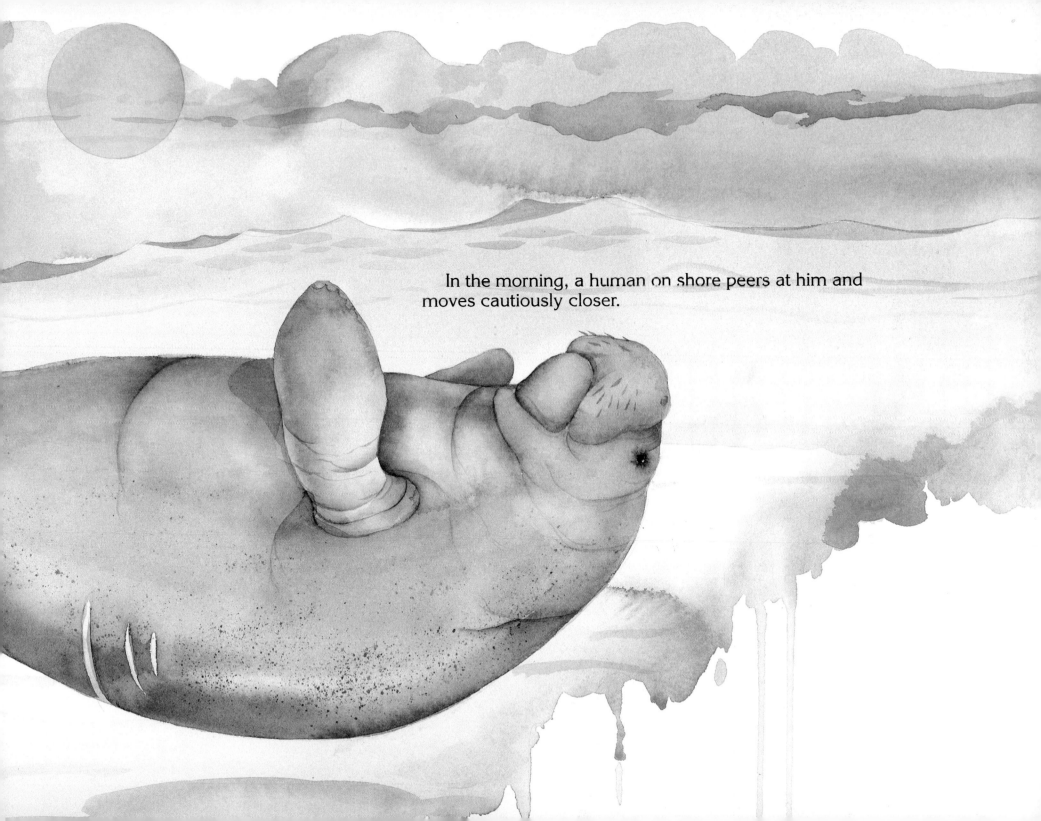

In the morning, a human on shore peers at him and moves cautiously closer.

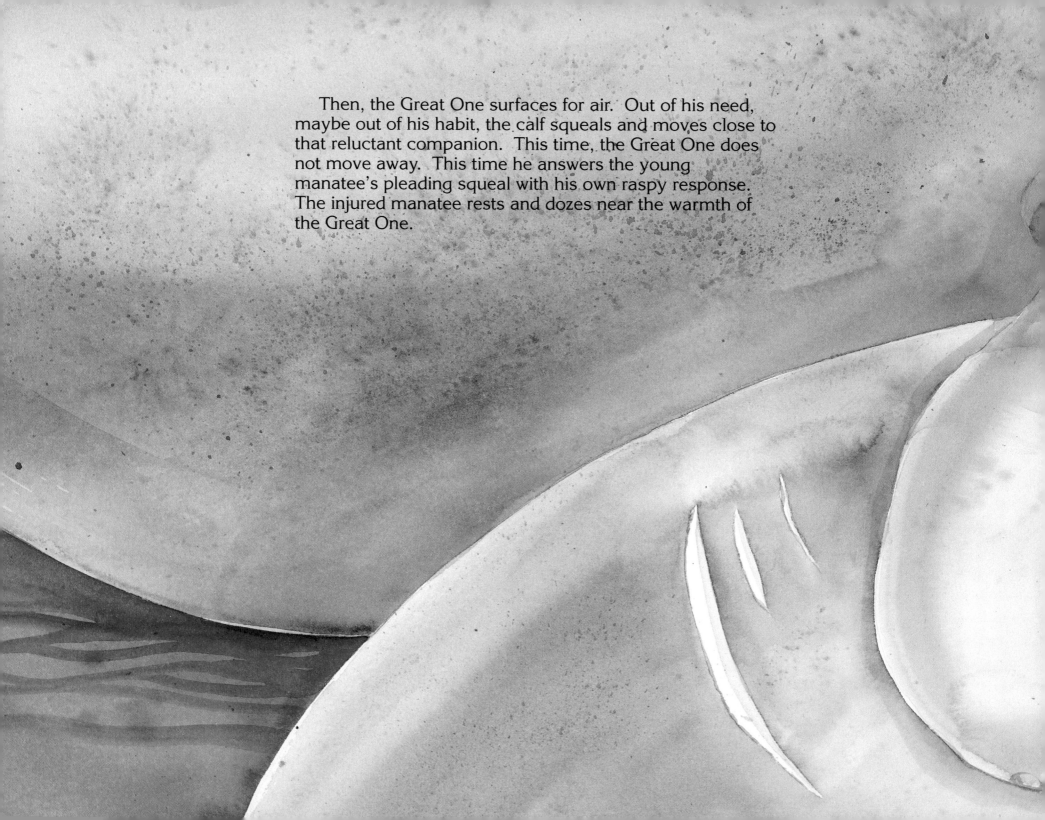

Then, the Great One surfaces for air. Out of his need, maybe out of his habit, the calf squeals and moves close to that reluctant companion. This time, the Great One does not move away. This time he answers the young manatee's pleading squeal with his own raspy response. The injured manatee rests and dozes near the warmth of the Great One.

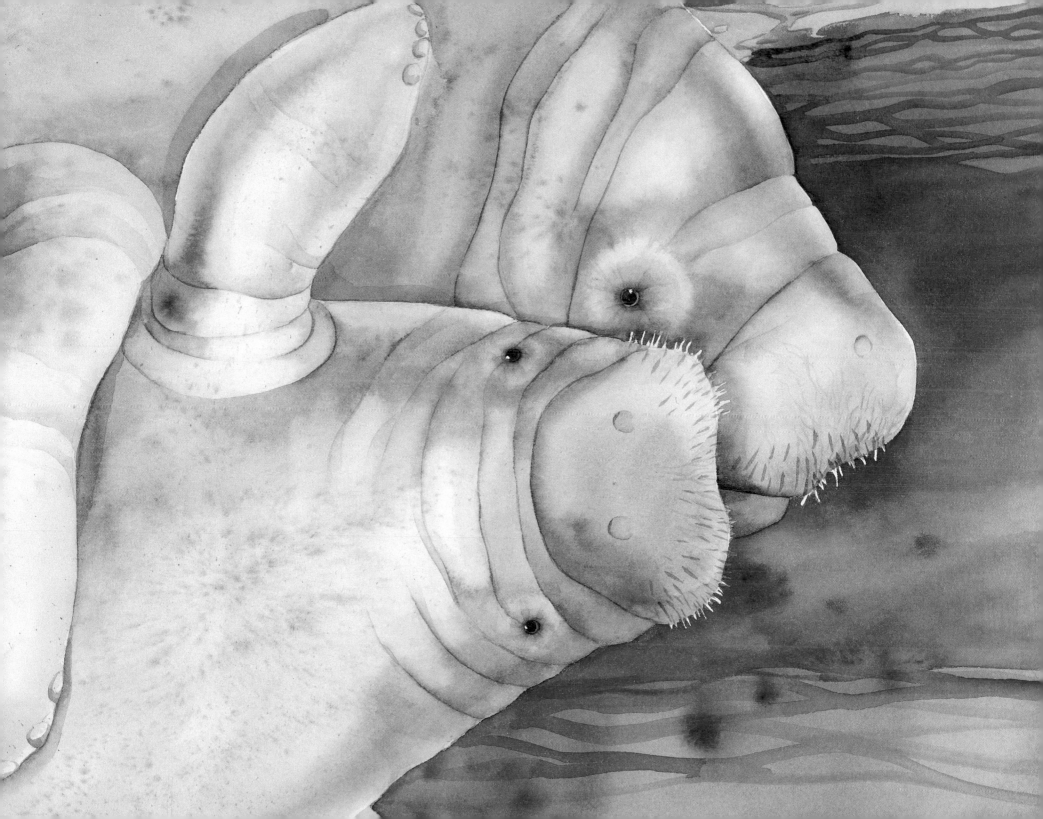

He is awakened later by the familiar sound of a motor. This is not a roar, but a drone. A large flat boat attempts to move between the injured manatee and his protector, but the Great One stays close to the calf. The young manatee's breathing has become painful and difficult, and he moves stiffly. A net is pitched from the back of the boat, almost entrapping him, but he painfully swims and avoids it. The Great One and the calf stay close together, but they cannot escape. The injured manatee is unable to plunge to the floor of the lagoon.

The young manatee grows more exhausted in his attempts to breathe. He squints in terror each time the net is hurled at him. Finally, the pontoon wedges between the two companions. The net flies at him again, and this time it traps him. He fights and rolls, but only becomes more entangled. He is too weak to fight any longer. Slowly he is dragged across the surface of the water to the distant shore.

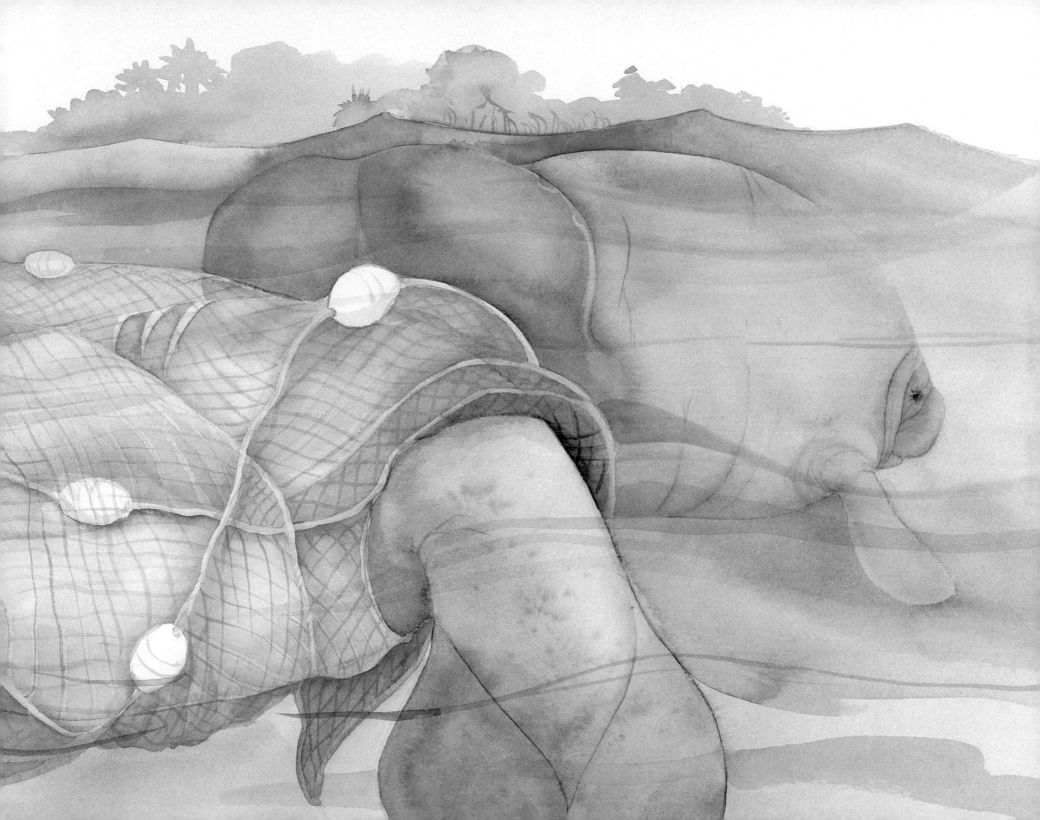

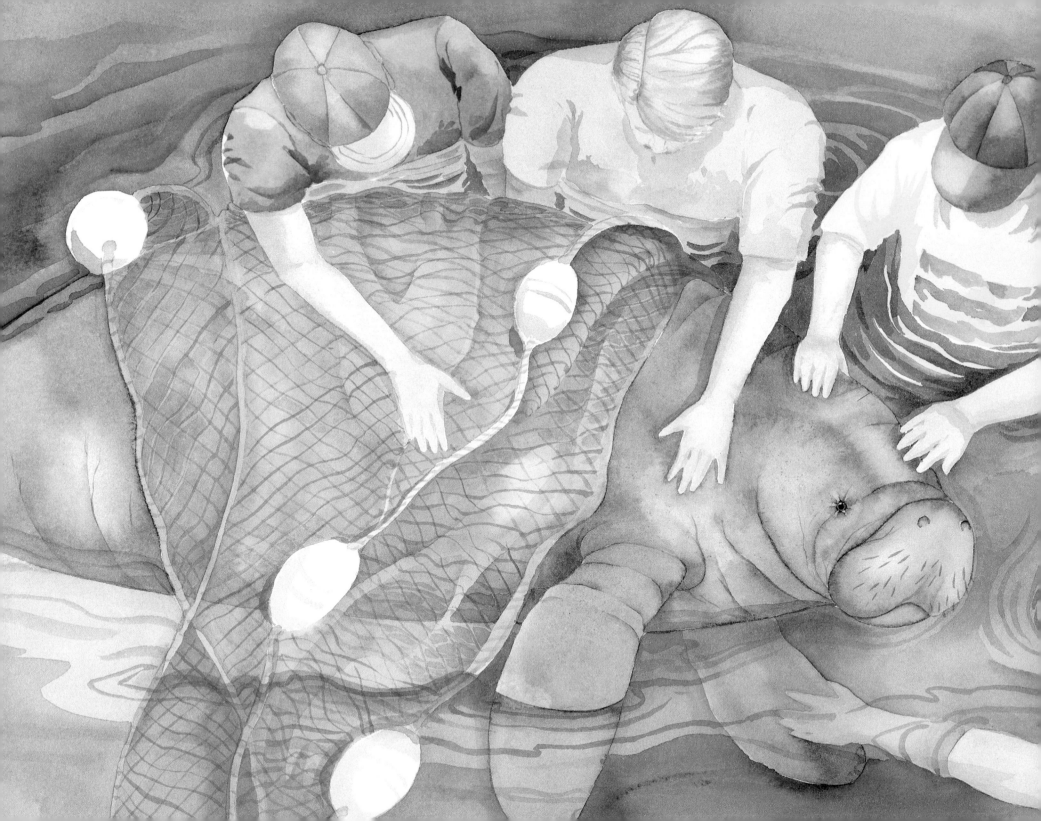

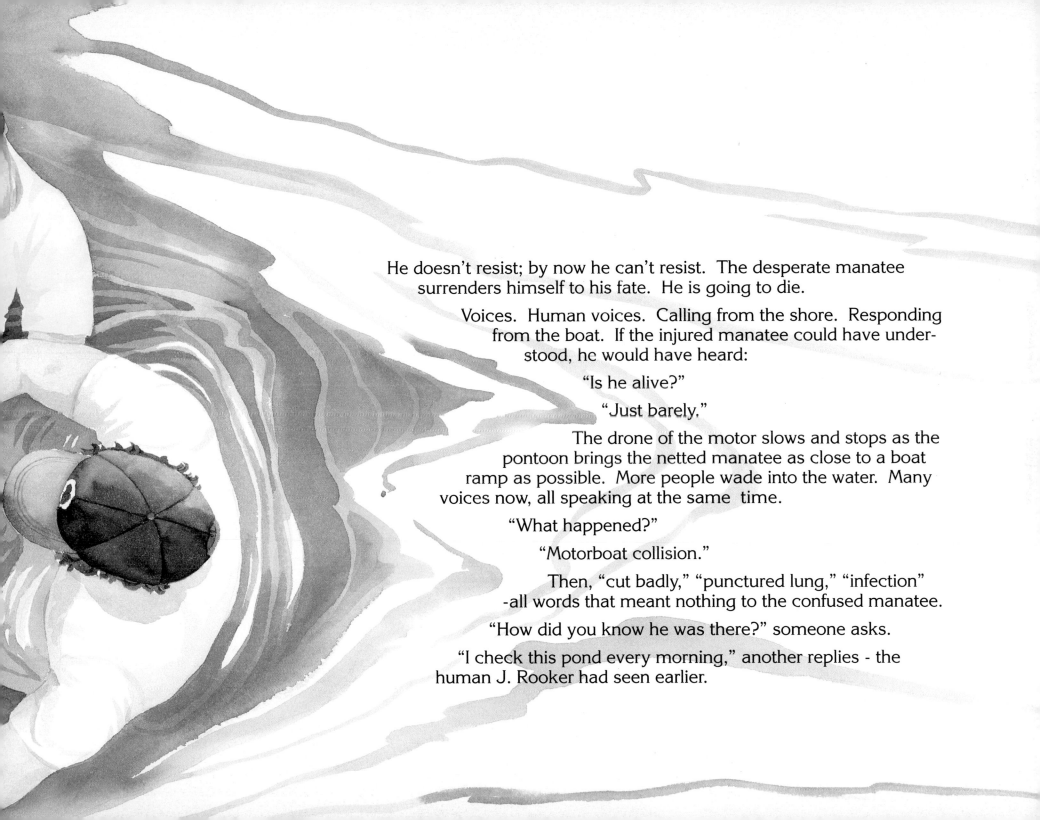

He doesn't resist; by now he can't resist. The desperate manatee surrenders himself to his fate. He is going to die.

Voices. Human voices. Calling from the shore. Responding from the boat. If the injured manatee could have understood, he would have heard:

"Is he alive?"

"Just barely."

The drone of the motor slows and stops as the pontoon brings the netted manatee as close to a boat ramp as possible. More people wade into the water. Many voices now, all speaking at the same time.

"What happened?"

"Motorboat collision."

Then, "cut badly," "punctured lung," "infection" -all words that meant nothing to the confused manatee.

"How did you know he was there?" someone asks.

"I check this pond every morning," another replies - the human J. Rooker had seen earlier.

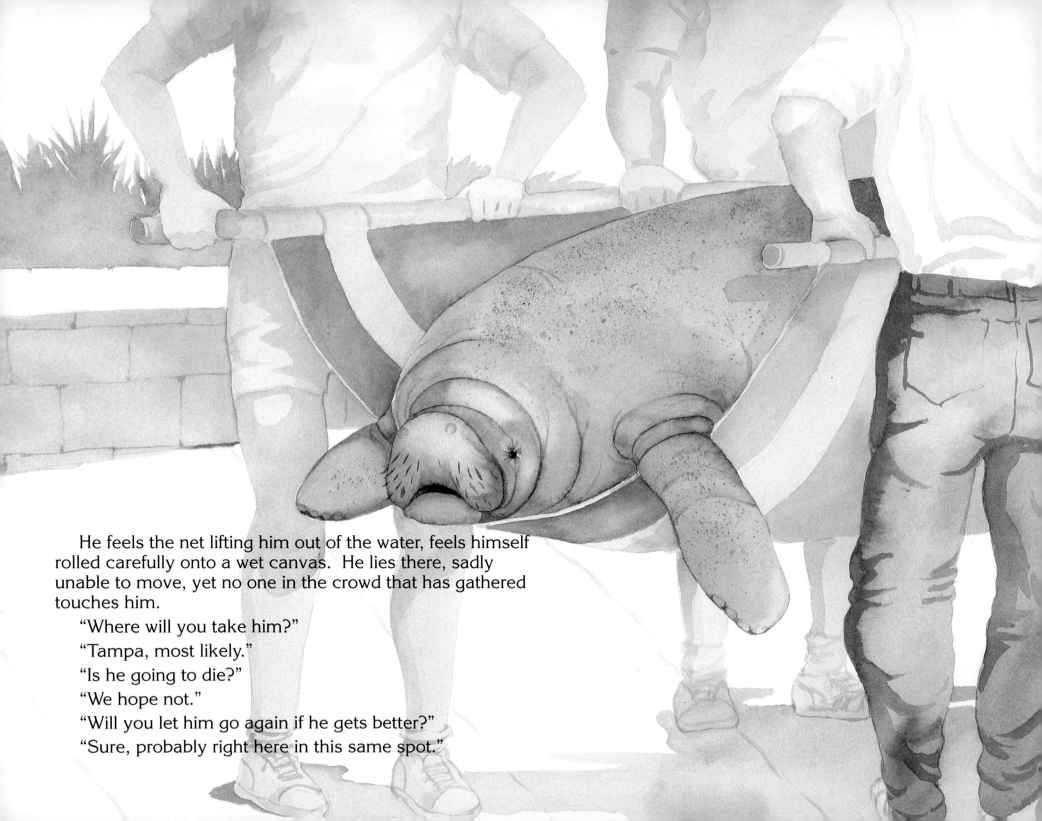

He feels the net lifting him out of the water, feels himself rolled carefully onto a wet canvas. He lies there, sadly unable to move, yet no one in the crowd that has gathered touches him.

"Where will you take him?"

"Tampa, most likely."

"Is he going to die?"

"We hope not."

"Will you let him go again if he gets better?"

"Sure, probably right here in this same spot."

A van backs slowly down the ramp. Two large doors
open wide, and more people climb out. The sides of the
strong canvas around him are lifted by rows of people.
The movement brings new spasms of pain to the young
manatee, and he shivers in the hot Florida sun.

"One, two, three, ho!" He is hoisted up into the van.

The sides of the canvas are folded over him, and he is
enveloped in darkness. Yes, this is death, he is certain;
and he slips into a deep sleep.

Lowry Park Zoo in Tampa is one of Florida's rehabilitation facilities for injured manatees. The injured manatee doesn't know that, but when he awakens, he has arrived at the zoo. He discovers that his wound is being treated. Upon examination and X-rays, the extent of his injuries is finally known. The young manatee is in critical condition.

He has four broken ribs on his right side. One of the broken ribs has punctured his right lung. Bones in his lower back have been twisted out of alignment, and he is suffering from infection. He is treated for his injuries and given antibiotics and vitamins to combat the infection and to build up his strength. He is placed in a quiet observation tank to begin the slow recovery.

He is given the name "J. Rooker," "J" for junior and "Rooker" for Rookery Bay, the place of his rescue. He eats food he has never tasted before - bean sprouts, carrots, and apples, and the romaine lettuce he learns to love. The humans are gentle. He learns to trust them. In seven months, he is ready to go home. He has gained 228 pounds.

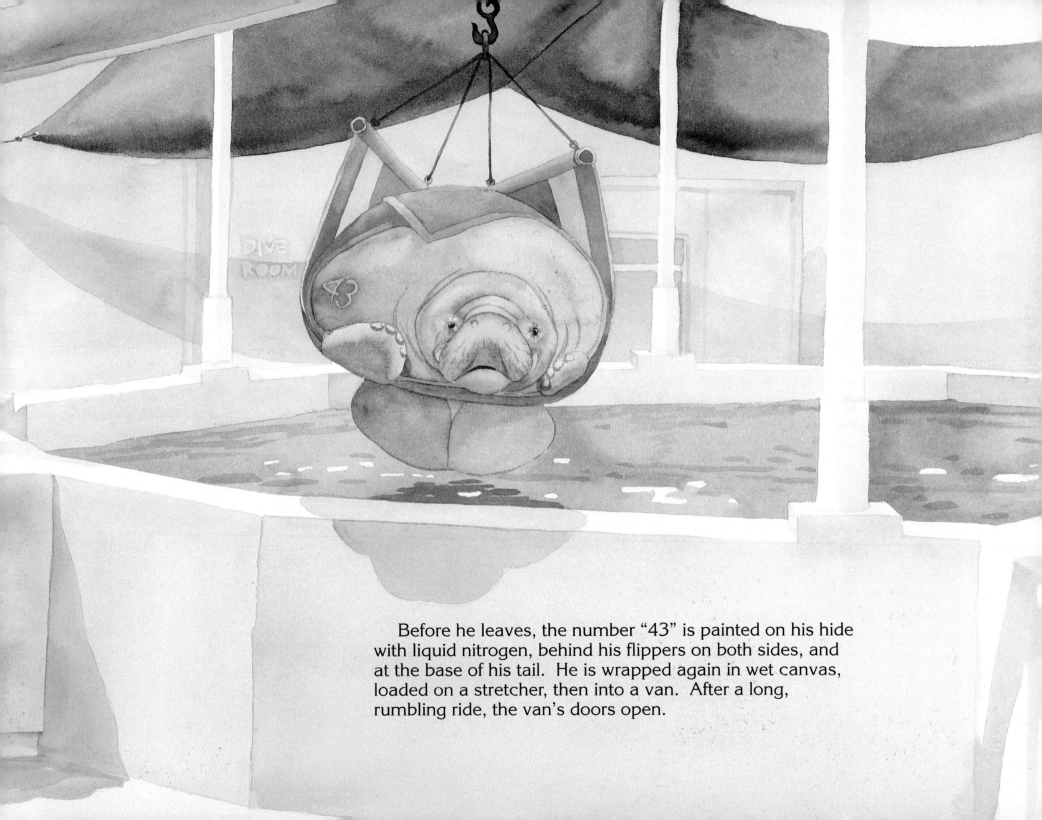

Before he leaves, the number "43" is painted on his hide with liquid nitrogen, behind his flippers on both sides, and at the base of his tail. He is wrapped again in wet canvas, loaded on a stretcher, then into a van. After a long, rumbling ride, the van's doors open.

He has returned to the point of his capture. He is placed gently in the water, as a crowd gathers to watch.

At first he doesn't leave, won't leave. A bond of friendship has developed between the manatee and his caretakers. The growing crowd of onlookers silently share feelings of compassion and connection. Long minutes pass.

"He doesn't want to leave," someone calls.

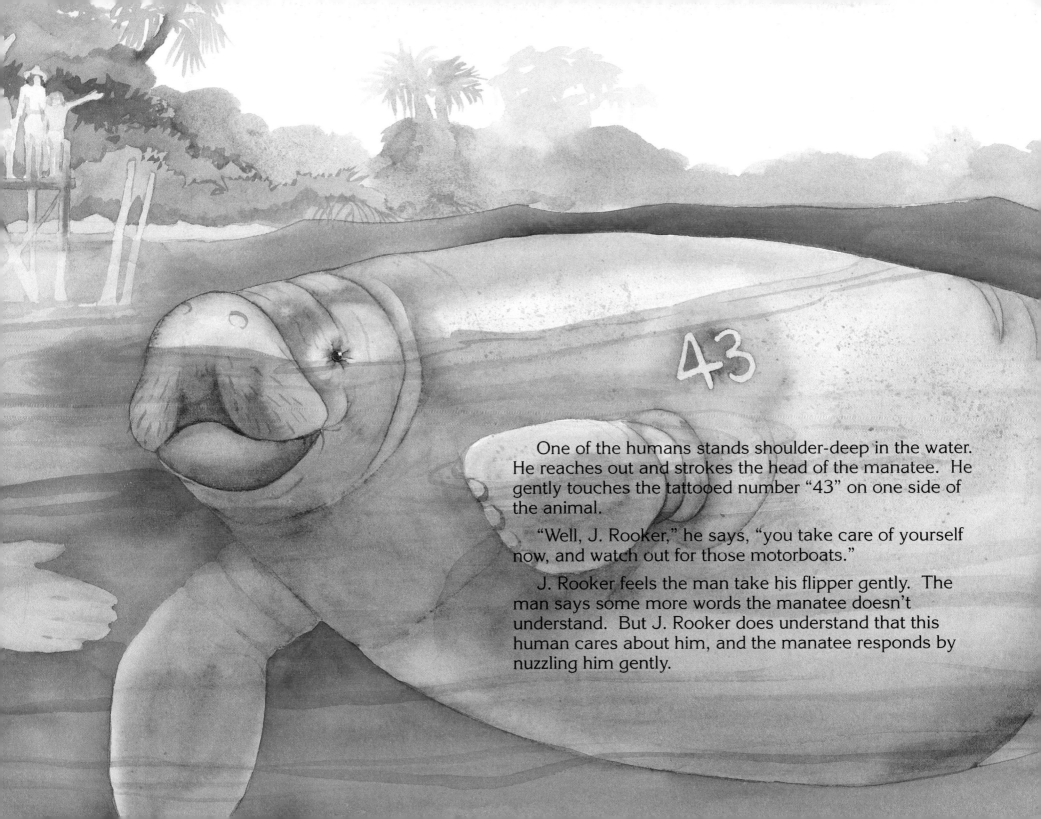

One of the humans stands shoulder-deep in the water. He reaches out and strokes the head of the manatee. He gently touches the tattooed number "43" on one side of the animal.

"Well, J. Rooker," he says, "you take care of yourself now, and watch out for those motorboats."

J. Rooker feels the man take his flipper gently. The man says some more words the manatee doesn't understand. But J. Rooker does understand that this human cares about him, and the manatee responds by nuzzling him gently.

Abruptly, J. Rooker paddles away. To the spectators behind him, he seems to disappear. They could never know that their young friend would soon find the Great One, waiting for him with welcome recognition. But J. Rooker could see that reunion in his mind's eye. He felt it quivering along his spine.

Home. He was going home.

More about Manatees

Manatees are marine mammals who can live in salt water or fresh water. They are plant-eating, air breathing animals who must rise to the surface every few minutes for air when swimming. When a manatee is resting on the bottom, he can stay there for 15 to 20 minutes before rising for breath. Manatees are warm-blooded and very sensitive to cold; staying warm requires most of their energy. A mature manatee may be as long as 15 feet and weigh 3,000 pounds; new-borns average about 75 pounds. Mature manatees eat over 100 pounds of aquatic roots and vegetation each day, and have been observed cleaning their teeth regularly after eating. They nurse their young.

Naturalists who study the behavior of manatees report that they communicate with one another with high-pitched squeals that become more scratchy sounding as they get older. They are sociable crea-tures who nuzzle each other and embrace with paddle-shaped flippers. Their flexible bodies stretch and twist broadly, and they are known to sigh in contentment as we do in relaxation.

The docile manatees are harmless to other crea-tures. They can live as long as 50 years in the wild. They have no natural predators. Their greatest enemy, however, is man.

Each year many manatees who have been wounded are rescued and rehabilitated. Whenever possible, they are returned to the sea once they have recovered. Others, who might not survive on their own, are sent to authorized marine parks where they are cared for and where they are introduced to people who are challenged to support efforts to save and protect their relatives back in the wild.

The 1978 Florida Manatee Sanctuary Act estab-lished the entire state as a Refuge and Sanctuary for Manatees. Despite this act, however, dredging, commercial development, and water pollution destroy more and more of the manatees' natural habitat each year, forcing them to seek refuge in man-made water-ways and lagoons where motorboat activity is high and other fishing paraphernalia snare and trap them. Many humans are too impatient to drive boats at no-wake speed, and the sluggish animals are often mangled by sharp propellers, probably far more often than we can know. Scientists have estimated that over half the manatees who die following boat strikes succumb to internal injuries caused by the impact of the boat's hull rather than from the visible cuts made by the boat's propeller.

These mammals are more intelligent than they look. Many have learned to move away from the roar of motorboats. A few swim close to the water's edge to avoid boats. Some manatees even reserve their activity to nighttime hours when their enemy is anchored.

Despite these adaptations, the death rate of manatees has outnumbered the birthrate for years. This downward spiral may mean that manatees could be extinct within our lifetime: Time is running out for them.

The U.S. Fish and Wildlife Service has ultimate authority over all endangered animals. However, Rookery Bay National Estuarine Research Reserve, (NERR) in Naples is one of southwest Florida's regional rescue and transport facilities for marine mammals, and has the authority to recover injured and dead marine mammals.

NERR staff member Steve Bertone monitors manatee activity in the lagoon near Henderson Creek daily. He facilitated the rescue of J. Rooker, with the help of Rookery Bay staff and volunteers. Manatees range great distances offshore to the north and back. Rookery Bay NERR is interested in learning further information about J. Rooker. If you are visiting the area, watch for a manatee bearing the number "43." The Rookery Bay Reserve phone number is (941) 775-8845.

Friends of Rookery Bay (FORB) is a volunteer-based, not-for-profit organization that aides the reserve. The cost of membership is nominal, and the rewards are great. A portion of the profits of this book are being donated to this organization.

Lowry Park Zoo in Tampa, Florida, has an excellent manatee rehabilitation facility. Manatee's favorite food in captivity is romaine lettuce. It costs $30,000 a year to feed one adult manatee in captivity, where their diet also includes cabbage, fish, and biscuits.

Lowry Park Zoo is privately funded. This means the Zoo depends on admission, food & gift sales and donations for operating costs. For more information on ways to help the Zoo or to send cash donations, here is their address: Lowry Park Zoo, 7530 North Boulevard, Tampa, FL 33604 or call (813) 935-8552.

The production of this book has been a collaborative effort, and we wish to thank Steven Bertone of NERR for his valuable technical knowledge, Lowry Park Zoo for their gracious information, and special recognition and gratitude to Sara Saetre for her gifted editing.

It is the purpose of this book to raise levels of awareness about the plight of manatees. Together we can work to protect them, so that we can continue to know these gentle giants of the sea.

Jan Haley
Paul Brent

Save The MANATEE Club

Save the Manatee Club (SMC) was established in 1981 so the general public could participate in conservation efforts to save manatees from extinction. The Adopt-A-Manatee program is the major public awareness effort sponsored by SMC. Twenty-two manatees who winter at Blue Spring State Park in Orange City, FL, and five manatees who live at Homosassa Springs State Wildlife Park in Florida have been chosen for the Adopt-A-Manatee program. Each member receives an adoption kit that includes a picture of their adopted manatee, the manatee's history, an adoption certificate, general information about manatees, and four newsletters per year.

The Adopt-A-Manatee program is the primary source of funding for SMC. Funds from the Adopt-A-Manatee program go toward public awareness and education, research, rescue and rehabilitation efforts, and lobbying, in order to ensure better protection for manatees and their habitat.

If you would like to find out more information about manatees, manatee curriculum material for educators, or the Adopt-A-Manatee program, write Save the Manatee Club at: 500 N. Maitland Ave., Maitland FL 32751, call 1-800-432-JOIN, or e-mail us at: manatee@america.com